SOUND the DEEP WATERS

Dear Polly

Wishing you a very Merry Christmas 1998

with love from

[illegible] xx

*

SOUND the DEEP WATERS

WOMEN'S ROMANTIC POETRY in the VICTORIAN AGE

Edited by
PAMELA NORRIS

TIGER BOOKS INTERNATIONAL

This edition published in 1998 by
Tiger Books International PLC, Twickenham, U.K.

First published in Great Britain in 1991 by
Little, Brown and Company (UK) Limited
Brettenham House, Lancaster Place
London WC2E 7EN

ISBN 1–84056–002–9

Decorative illustrations by Nadine Wickenden
Design by David Fordham

Printed in Italy

Contents

Dreams and Realities

Last Songs

~INTRODUCTION~

'Man for the field and woman for the hearth:
Man for the sword and for the needle she:
Man with the head and woman with the heart:
Man to command and woman to obey;
All else confusion.'

The words of the old king in Tennyson's 'The Princess' sum up the prevailing Victorian view of the appropriate role for women. In Coventry Patmore's hugely popular poem, 'The Angel in the House', the ideal wife is described as a domestic saint, whose purity and goodness protect the home – and her husband – against the grossness of the outside world.

The Victorians liked their women to be angels and they preferred them to be based very firmly in the home. A consequence, or perhaps a result, of this focus on woman's domestic role was that practical or creative work outside the home came to be considered degrading or too stressful for middle-class women. At the same time, these women generally had servants to care for their children and cope with the physical drudgery required to maintain their often substantial households. Apart from charity work, or governessing for those in straitened circumstances, middle-class women were expected to devote themselves to their husbands, children and social lives, and to the pursuit of elegant and well-groomed leisure. Inexpert strumming on the piano, delicate watercolour paintings of flowers, or making shell-boxes were considered desirable ways of filling the long hours between breakfast and bedtime. A little light reading was also approved, suitable to women's less well-developed mental faculties.

But what did women themselves want from their lives? Were they happy to be subservient to the male members of the household? And how did they feel about focusing their energies on their families and undemanding hobbies rather than making a serious attempt to develop their own interests and abilities? The poets represented in *Sound the Deep Waters* suggest, both in their lives and

their poetry, that for some women at least the reality was rather different from the popular stereotype.

One myth that their lives explode is that of the comfortable home supported by the male breadwinner: there was considerable variety in the living circumstances of these writers. The three Brontë sisters, outspoken advocates in their fiction of woman's right to determine her own fate, lived for most of their lives with their father in the secluded parsonage at Haworth. Financial hardship drove them outside the home at various periods to study or work as governesses; and their brief lives were marked by poverty, domestic toil and hard creative effort, with powerful, often heroic feelings struggling for expression within the narrow boundaries of their external circumstances. The poems included in this anthology demonstrate different aspects of their personalities: Charlotte's moods of quiet meditation, Anne's simple response to nature and human feeling, and Emily's uncompromising claim to emotions that would generally have been regarded as unwomanly or even sacrilegious.

Like Charlotte Brontë, Elizabeth Barrett Browning married comparatively late in life, dramatically running away from her demanding father to live in Italy with the poet Robert Browning, bearing their son when she was already 43, and continuing to be a productive poet for several happy years before her death. However, her more affluent family circumstances meant that, unlike the Brontës, Elizabeth had been free to devote her energies singleheartedly to her writing. Largely self-taught, she made a point of mastering knowledge that was customarily a male prerogative and her intelligence and learning are expressed in the large body of poetry she published. But she was also mistress of what Tennyson's king designated the female domain of the emotions: 'Grief', included in this anthology, explores the immobilising effect of intense suffering, well-illustrated by Anna Lea Merritt's accompanying painting 'War', where the dominant female figure seems frozen by the impact of the news of the soldiers in the street below.

Marriage and the need to house and feed a growing troop of children provided the incentive for many women to write for publication. Edith Nesbit was a prolific writer of verse before she established herself as a successful novelist for children. In the early years of her marriage to fellow Fabian Herbert Bland, their expanding household (which included two of his 'love' children and their mother) largely relied on Edith's pen for the lentil and bean dishes with which she nourished her dependents when times were hard. Alice Meynell also wrote to support an extensive family. Other writers, however, remained resolutely single. Christina Rossetti evaded two offers of marriage to live quietly at home with her beloved mother, writing her poems in a little back room in moments

of leisure from household duties and her charitable work for 'fallen' women. The American poet, Emily Dickinson, was even more reclusive, establishing her right to retire from family life as often as she chose and writing literally hundreds of poems which she kept hidden away in trunks and drawers.

The subject matter of the poems in *Sound the Deep Waters* reflects the different interests and experiences of the poets. As is seen in the section 'Love's Bitter-Sweets', love was a favourite topic, but the experiences described were not always happy, an ambivalence pinpointed in Emily Brontë's comparison of love with the wild rose-briar, which withers so unattractively in the wintertime. Christina Rossetti's 'A Birthday' celebrates joyous meeting with the beloved; in 'Echo' she bitterly laments lost love. In 'Go From Me', a sonnet written to celebrate her love for her future husband, Elizabeth Barrett Browning describes the colonising power of love: 'What I do / And what I dream include thee, as the wine / Must taste of its own grapes.' Emma Lazarus's 'The Elixir' and Lizette Woodworth Reese's 'The Singer' remind us of the interest in romantic mediaevalism during the period, which was reflected in its paintings.

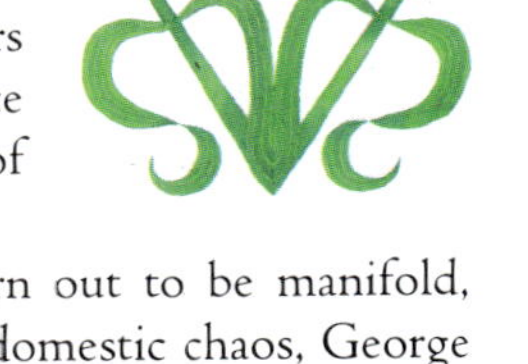

Death, explored in 'Last Songs', was also a favourite theme, perhaps not surprisingly at a period of both high infant mortality and an adult lifespan that was frequently shorter than is the norm today. The message of Dora Sigerson Shorter's 'The Watcher in the Wood' is the inevitability of death, while others write poignantly of mourning, perhaps none more pathetically than Alice Meynell in 'Maternity', a fragment lamenting the traumatic stunting of maternal impulses that inevitably accompanies the loss of a child.

'Moments of Delight', however, celebrate life's pleasures, which turn out to be manifold, including Dollie Radford's daring indulgence of a cigarette in the midst of domestic chaos, George Eliot's fond memories of childhood fishing expeditions with her brother, and the rich enjoyment of nature in poems such as Anne Brontë's 'A Windy Day' and Helen Jackson's 'Poppies on the Wheat'. Edith Nesbit's 'Morning Song' presents the happier side of motherhood.

'Dreams and Realities' explore what might be termed 'philosophies': the poets' attempts to read meaning and pattern into life. George Eliot's rhapsodic account of conventional love and marriage, 'Two Lovers', contrasts with the harsh realism of Mary Elizabeth Coleridge's 'The Other Side of a Mirror', where a woman gazes aghast at the horrific reflection of her true self. Christina Rossetti also writes about mirrors in 'Passing and Glassing', but metaphorically – the natural world is replete with reminders of the transience of human life and its vanities. Her eloquently simple 'Up-hill' concludes this section with a comforting glimpse of the welcome and peace at the end of life's often laborious path.

'Sound the deep waters', the title of the anthology, is the first line of another poem by Christina Rossetti. Too long to be included in the collection, 'Sleep at Sea' describes a ship full of dreaming sailors, immune to the frantic attempts of warning spirits to recall them to their duties in the real world, as their ship races ever forward through gigantic rocks to the tempest ahead. In this poem, dreams are seen as inimical to man's spiritual salvation: lost in pleasant reverie, he is heedless of the need to take control of the ship of life, which for Christina meant taking care of the soul's well-being.

In the poems by Victorian women in this anthology, there is an abundance of dreams, but the poets do not neglect to sound the deep waters of everyday life: its joys and pains and duties. Paradoxically, in many of the paintings that accompany these poems, while the artist's goal was visual realism, the subject matter was frequently drawn from mythology or old romance. In 1848 seven young men started a new artistic movement in revolt against what they criticised as the trite conventions of Establishment art. Known as the Pre-Raphaelite Brotherhood, the group included William Holman Hunt, John Everett Millais and two of Christina Rossetti's brothers: the artist and poet Dante Gabriel Rossetti and the critic William Michael Rossetti. The later history and development of the movement is complex, but its characteristics can be summarised as the choice of serious or highminded subject matter, 'natural' or realistic depiction of images, brilliant colour, and an accretion of symbolic detail. As well as 'real-life' subjects, stories from Keats, Tennyson and the early Italian poets, and from mediaeval legend were richly and imaginatively realised, as in Holman Hunt's 'Isabella and the Pot of Basil' (Keats) and Millais' 'Mariana in the Moated Grange' (Tennyson). Dante Gabriel Rossetti developed his own interpretation of the Brotherhood's tenets in exquisitely romantic and idealised representations of women: a brooding 'Proserpine' seconds after she has sampled the pomegranate seeds that will condemn her to six months' underground each year as Pluto's bride, a typically pensive maiden in 'Reverie', the lush imagery of 'The Beloved' and 'La Ghirlandata'. Different strands developed from the Brotherhood's initial impetus for change: see, for example, the works by Burne-Jones and John William Waterhouse. Other styles of painting continued to flourish alongside the Pre-Raphaelites throughout the Victorian period and are briefly indicated in *Sound the Deep Waters* by such works as Thomas Cooper Gotch's highly individual 'The Child Enthroned', and the delightful portraits of children and young women by the Anglo-French artist Sophie Anderson.

As we have seen with the poets, Victorian women artists also

confounded the female stereotypes and, despite the difficulty of acquiring adequate training or unpatronising display and evaluation of their work, were increasingly successful not only in developing their abilities as painters but in securing some degree of public recognition for their work. Many of the artists selected for inclusion in these pages were directly connected with or influenced by the Pre-Raphaelite movement. Marie Stillman (née Spartali) was a noted 'stunner' (the Pre-Raphaelite slang for a goodlooking woman) and sat for Rossetti and Burne-Jones as well as the photographer Julia Margaret Cameron. She studied with Ford Madox Brown along with his daughters Catherine and Lucy, and her watercolours were often inspired by the Italian poets: 'By a Clear Well, Within a Little Field' illustrates Rossetti's translation of a sonnet by Boccaccio. The Birmingham artist, Kate Elizabeth Bunce, was also influenced by Rossetti both in style and in subject matter. 'The Chance Meeting' captures a momentary contact between the Italian poet Dante and his beloved Beatrice. 'Undine' is probably the work of Louisa Starr, who became the first female gold medallist at the Royal Academy Schools in 1867. It offers a variation on the classic tale of the supernatural maiden, in this case a water nymph, who marries a human to acquire a soul. Predictably Undine is deserted for an earthly lover and appears at a suitably inappropriate moment, veiled as a bride and wringing her hands with despair as she claims the life of her faithless husband.

Among the most striking of the artists in these pages is Evelyn de Morgan (née Pickering). Groomed by her wealthy family for marriage, she studied art in secret until reluctantly allowed to attend the Slade School of Art. She went on to develop a career of distinction, and works such as 'Queen Eleanor and Fair Rosamund', 'Port after Stormy Seas' and 'The Prisoner' display her originality, love of colour, detail and pictorial symbolism, and her interest in neo-classical as well as traditionally Pre-Raphaelite subjects. 'Flora', painted in Florence and clearly influenced by Botticelli's 'Primavera', is particularly fine. 'The Worship of Mammon' exhibits a characteristic interest in moral issues.

As this brief Introduction suggests, there was considerably more to life for the Victorian woman than Tennyson's old king was prepared to allow. The poems in *Sound the Deep Waters* offer an insight into women's lives through the ideas, images and emotions they expressed in words; the paintings that accompany the poems suggest the dream worlds that played so important a role in Victorian culture, and to which both men and women made their individual and complex contributions, as writers, artists and fellow travellers through the sixty-odd years of Victoria's reign.

Pamela Norris, Rye 1991

LOVE'S BITTER-SWEETS

Love is like the wild rose-briar;

EMILY JANE BRONTË

HYLAS AND THE NYMPHS,
John William Waterhouse.

LOVE and FRIENDSHIP

Love is like the wild rose-briar;
  Friendship like the holly-tree.
The holly is dark when the rose-briar blooms,
  But which will bloom most constantly?

The wild rose-briar is sweet in spring,
  Its summer blossoms scent the air;
Yet wait till winter comes again,
  And who will call the wild-briar fair?

Then, scorn the silly rose-wreath now,
  And deck thee with the holly's sheen,
That, when December blights thy brow,
  He still may leave thy garland green.

EMILY JANE BRONTË

QUEEN ELEANOR AND FAIR ROSAMUND, *Evelyn de Morgan*

JOLIE COEUR, (after Rossetti), *Marie Spartali Stillman.*

A LOVE TOKEN

Do you grieve no costly offering
To the Lady you can make?
One there is, and gifts less worthy
Queens have stooped to take.

Take a Heart of virgin silver,
Fashion it with heavy blows,
Cast it into Love's hot furnace
When it fiercest glows.

With Pain's sharpest point transfix it,
And then carve in letters fair,
Tender dreams and quaint devices,
Fancies sweet and rare.

Set within it Hope's blue sapphire,
Many-changing opal fears,
Blood-red ruby-stones of daring,
Mixed with pearly tears.

And when you have wrought and laboured
Till the gift is all complete,
You may humbly lay your offering
At the Lady's feet.

Should her mood perchance be gracious –
With disdainful smiling pride,
She will place it with the trinkets
Glittering at her side.

ADELAIDE ANNE PROCTER

Go from Me

Go from me. Yet I feel that I shall stand
Henceforward in thy shadow. Nevermore
Alone upon the threshold of my door
Of individual life, I shall command
The uses of my soul, nor lift my hand
Serenely in the sunshine as before,
Without the sense of that which I forebore –
Thy touch upon the palm. The widest land
Doom takes to part us, leaves thy heart in mine
With pulses that beat double. What I do
And what I dream include thee, as the wine
Must taste of its own grapes. And when I sue
God for myself, He hears that name of thine,
And sees within my eyes the tears of two.

No. VI of 'Sonnets from the Portuguese'

Elizabeth Barrett Browning

THE CHANCE MEETING, *Kate Elizabeth Bunce.*

UNDINE, *attributed to Louisa Starr Canziani.*

The Long White Seam

As I came round the harbour buoy,
The lights began to gleam,
No wave the land-locked water stirred,
The crags were white as cream;
And I marked my love by candle-light
Sewing her long white seam.
It's aye sewing ashore, my dear,
Watch and steer at sea,
It's reef and furl, and haul the line,
Set sail and think of thee.

I climbed to reach her cottage door;
O sweetly my love sings!
Like a shaft of light her voice breaks forth,
My soul to meet it springs
As the shining water leaped of old,
When stirred by angel wings.
Aye longing to list anew,
Awake and in my dream,
But never a song she sang like this,
Sewing her long white seam.

Fair fall the lights, the harbour lights,
That brought me in to thee,
And peace drop down on that low roof
For the sight that I did see,
And the voice, my dear, that rang so clear
All for the love of me.
For O, for O, with brows bent low
By the candle's flickering gleam,
Her wedding gown it was she wrought,
Sewing the long white seam.

JEAN INGELOW

WILD NIGHTS

Wild Nights – Wild Nights!
Were I with thee
Wild Nights should be
Our luxury!

Futile – the Winds –
To a Heart in port –
Done with the Compass –
Done with the Chart!

Rowing in Eden –
Ah, the Sea!
Might I but moor – Tonight –
In Thee!

EMILY DICKINSON

PORT AFTER STORMY SEAS, *Evelyn de Morgan.*

THE KEEPSAKE, *Kate Elizabeth Bunce.*

A BIRTHDAY

My heart is like a singing bird
 Whose nest is in a watered shoot;
My heart is like an appletree
 Whose boughs are bent with thickset fruit;
My heart is like a rainbow shell
 That paddles in a halcyon sea;
My heart is gladder than all these
 Because my love is come to me.

Raise me a dais of silk and down;
 Hang it with vair and purple dyes;
Carve it in doves, and pomegranates,
 And peacocks with a hundred eyes;
Work it in gold and silver grapes,
 In leaves, and silver fleurs-de-lys;
Because the birthday of my life
 Is come, my love is come to me.

Christina Rossetti

The MOUNTAIN MAID

Half seated on a mossy crag,
Half crouching in the heather;
I found a little Irish maid,
All in June's golden weather.

Like some fond hand that loved the child,
The wind tossed back her tresses;
The heath-bells touched her unclad feet
With shy and soft caresses.

A mountain linnet flung his song
Into the air around her;
But all in vain the splendid hour,
For deep in woe I found her.

'Ahone! Ahone! Ahone!' she wept,
The tears fell fast and faster;
I sat myself beside her there,
To hear of her disaster.

Like dew on roses down her cheek
The diamond drops were stealing;
She laid her two brown hands in mine,
Her trouble all revealing.

Alas! Alas! the tale she told
In Gaelic low and tender;
A plague upon my Saxon tongue,
I could not comprehend her.

DORA SIGERSON SHORTER

YOUNG GIRL WITH A GARLAND OF MARGUERITES, *Sophie Anderson.*

The ELIXIR

'Oh brew me a potion strong and good!
    One golden drop in his wine
Shall charm his sense and fire his blood,
    And bend his will to mine.'

Poor child of passion! ask of me
    Elixir of death or sleep,
Or Lethe's stream; but love is free,
    And woman must wait and weep.

Emma Lazarus

MORGAN-LE-FAY, *Anthony Frederick Sandys.*

THE LAMENT, *Edward Burne-Jones.*

The SINGER

With spices, wines, and silken stuffs,
The stout ship sailed down,
And with the ship the singer came
Unto the old sea town.

'Peace to ye!' quoth the sailor folk,
'A month and more have we
Been listening to his songs. Ah, God!
None sings so sweet as he.'

Up from the wharves the salt wind blew,
And filled the steep highway;
Seven slender plum trees caught the sun
Within a courtyard gray.

Out came the daughter of the king;
Oh, very fair was she!
She was the whitest bough a-grow,
So fair, so fair was she!

The singer sang, 'My love,' he sang,
'Is like a white plum-tree!'
Then silence fell on house and court;
No other word sang he.

The king's daughter, when she was old,
Sat in a broidered gown,
And spun the flax from her fair fields –
Oh, it was sweet in town!

Seven plum-trees stood down in the court,
Each one was white as milk;
The king's daughter rose softly there,
Rustling her broidered silk.

'Oh, set the wheel away, my maids,
And sing that song to me
The singer sang!' 'My love,' sang they,
'Is like a white plum-tree!'

Lizette Woodworth Reese

ECHO

Come to me in the silence of the night;
    Come in the speaking silence of a dream;
Come with soft rounded cheeks and eyes as bright
    As sunlight on a stream;
        Come back in tears,
O memory, hope, love of finished years.

Oh dream how sweet, too sweet, too bitter sweet,
    Whose wakening should have been in Paradise,
Where souls brimfull of love abide and meet;
    Where thirsting longing eyes
        Watch the slow door
That opening, letting in, lets out no more.

Yet come to me in dreams, that I may live
    My very life again though cold in death:
Come back to me in dreams, that I may give
    Pulse for pulse, breath for breath:
        Speak low, lean low,
As long ago, my love, how long ago!

Christina Rossetti

LOVE'S PASSING, *Evelyn de Morgan.*

MELODY (MUSICA), *Kate Elizabeth Bunce.*

A SHATTERED LUTE

I touched the heart that loved me as a player
    Touches a lyre. Content with my poor skill,
    No touch save mine knew my beloved (and still
I thought at times: Is there no sweet lost air

Old loves could wake in him, I cannot share?)
    O he alone, alone could so fulfil
    My thoughts in sound to the measure of my will.
He is gone, and silence takes me unaware.

The songs I knew not he resumes, set free
From my constraining love, alas for me!
    His part in our tune goes with him; my part

Is locked in me for ever; I stand as mute
    As one with vigorous music in his heart
Whose fingers stray upon a shattered lute.

Alice Meynell

HORA STELLATRIX

The stars hang thick in the apple tree,
The south wind smells of the pungent sea,
Gold tulip cups are heavy with dew.
The night's for you, Sweetheart, for you!
Starfire rains from the vaulted blue.

Listen! The dancing of unseen leaves.
A drowsy swallow stirs in the eaves.
Only a maiden is sorrowing.
'T is night and spring, Sweetheart, and spring!
Starfire lights your heart's blossoming.

In the intimate dark there's never an ear,
Though the tulips stand on tiptoe to hear,
So give; ripe fruit must shrivel or fall.
As you are mine, Sweetheart, give all!
Starfire sparkles, your coronal.

AMY LOWELL

LUX IN TENEBRIS, *Evelyn de Morgan.*

MOMENTS of DELIGHT

My soul is awakened, my spirit is soaring

ANNE BRONTË

SPRING (APPLE BLOSSOMS),
John Everett Millais.

THE STORM SPIRITS, *Evelyn de Morgan.*

A WINDY DAY

My soul is awakened, my spirit is soaring
And carried aloft on the wings of the breeze;
For above and around me the wild wind is roaring,
Arousing to rapture the earth and the seas.

The long withered grass in the sunshine is glancing,
The bare trees are tossing their branches on high;
The dead leaves, beneath them, are merrily dancing,
The white clouds are scudding across the blue sky.

I wish I could see how the ocean is lashing
The foam of its billows to whirlwinds of spray;
I wish I could see how its proud waves are dashing,
And hear the wild roar of their thunder to-day!

ANNE BRONTË

A NECKLACE OF WILD FLOWERS, *Emma Sandys.*

The BEST THING in the WORLD

What's the best thing in the world?
June-rose, by May-dew impearled;
Sweet south-wind, that means no rain;
Truth, not cruel to a friend;
Pleasure, not in haste to end;
Beauty, not self-decked and curled
Till its pride is over-plain;
Light, that never makes you wink;
Memory, that gives no pain;
Love, when, *so*, you're loved again.
What's the best thing in the world?
– Something out of it, I think.

Elizabeth Barrett Browning

MORNING SONG

Baby darling, wake and see,
Morning's here, my little rose;
Open eyes and smile at me
Ere I clasp and kiss you close.
Baby darling, smile! for then
Mother sees the sun again.

Baby darling, sleep no more!
All the other flowers have done
With their sleeping – you, my flower,
Are the only sleepy one;
All the pink-frilled daisies shout:
'Bring our little sister out!'

Baby darling, in the sun
Birds are singing, sweet and shrill;
And my bird's the only one
That is nested softly still.
Baby – if you only knew,
All the birds are calling you!

Baby darling, all is bright,
God has brought the sunshine here;
And the sleepy silent night
Comes back soon enough, my dear!
Wake, my darling, night is done,
Sunbeams call my little one!

EDITH NESBIT

OURE LADYE OF GOOD CHILDREN, *Ford Madox Brown.*

THE PRISONER, *Evelyn de Morgan.*

POPPIES on the WHEAT

Along Ancona's hills the shimmering heat,
A tropic tide of air with ebb and flow
Bathes all the fields of wheat until they glow
Like flashing seas of green, which toss and beat
Around the vines. The poppies lithe and fleet
Seem running, fiery torchmen, to and fro
To mark the shore.
The farmer does not know
That they are there. He walks with heavy feet,
Counting the bread and wine by autumn's gain,
But I, – I smile to think that days remain
Perhaps to me in which, though bread be sweet
No more, and red wine warm my blood in vain,
I shall be glad remembering how the fleet,
Lithe poppies ran like torchmen with the wheat.

HELEN JACKSON

PEEK-A-BOO!, *Sophie Anderson.*

BLACKBERRY BLOSSOMS

Long sunny lane and pike, white, delicate,
The blackberry blossoms are ablow, ablow,
Hiding the rough-hewn rails 'neath drift of snow,
Fresh-fallen, late. The opening pasture gate
Brushes a hundred of them loose, and shakes
Them down into the tall delicious grass:
Sometimes a little sudden wind doth pass,
And all the air is full of flying flakes.
It seems but yesterday they blew as sweet
Down old school ways, and thrilled me with delight;
And reaching out for them, I heard the fleet,
Glad creek go spinning o'er its pebbles bright.
Ah, well! Ah, me! Even now, long as they last,
I am a child again; Joy holds me fast.

LIZETTE WOODWORTH REESE

I TASTE a LIQUOR

I taste a liquor never brewed –
From Tankards scooped in Pearl –
Not all the Vats upon the Rhine
Yield such an Alcohol!

Inebriate of Air – am I –
And Debauchee of Dew –
Reeling – thro endless summer days –
From inns of Molten Blue –

When 'Landlords' turn the drunken Bee
Out of the Foxglove's door –
When Butterflies – renounce their 'drams' –
I shall but drink the more!

Till Seraphs swing their snowy Hats –
And Saints – to windows run –
To see the little Tippler
Leaning against the – Sun –

EMILY DICKINSON

THE SENSE OF SIGHT, *Annie Swynnerton.*

BROTHER and SISTER

Long years have left their writing on my brow,
But yet the freshness and the dew-fed beam
Of those young mornings are about me now,
When we two wandered toward the far-off stream

With rod and line. Our basket held a store
Baked for us only, and I thought with joy
That I should have my share, though he had more,
Because he was the elder and a boy.

The firmaments of daisies since to me
Have had those mornings in their opening eyes,
The bunched cowslip's pale transparency
Carries that sunshine of sweet memories,

And wild-rose branches take their finest scent
From those blest hours of infantine content.

No. II of the 'Brother and Sister' sequence

George Eliot

HEAD OF A NYMPH, *Sophie Anderson.*

The AUTUMN DAY its COURSE has RUN

The Autumn day its course has run. The Autumn evening falls
Already risen the Autumn moon gleams quiet on these walls
And Twilight to my lonely house a silent guest is come
In mask of gloom through every room she passes dusk and dumb
Her veil is spread, her shadow shed o'er stair and chamber void
And now I feel her presence steal even to my lone fireside
Sit silent Nun – sit there and be
Comrade and Confidant to me

CHARLOTTE BRONTË

MARIANA IN THE MOATED GRANGE, *John Everett Millais.*

IL DOLCE FAR NIENTE, *William Holman Hunt.*

A NOVICE

What is it, in these latter days,
Transfigures my domestic ways,
And round me, as a halo, plays?
My cigarette.

For me so daintily prepared,
No modern skill, or perfume, spared,
What would have happened had I dared
To pass it yet?

What else could lighten times of woe,
When someone says 'I told you so,'
When all the servants, in a row,
Give notices?

When the great family affairs
Demand the most gigantic cares,
And one is very ill upstairs,
With poultices?

What else could ease my aching head,
When, though I long to be in bed,
I settle steadily instead
To my 'accounts?'

And while the house is slumbering,
Go over them like anything,
And find them ever varying,
In their amounts!

Ah yes, the cook may spoil the broth,
The cream of life resolve to froth,
I cannot now, though very wroth,
Distracted be;

For as the smoke curls blue and thin
From my own lips, I first begin
To bathe my tired spirit in
Philosophy.

And sweetest healing on her pours,
Once more into the world she soars,
And sees it full of open doors,
And helping hands.

In spite of those who, knocking, stay
At sullen portals day by day,
And weary at the long delay
To their demands.

The promised epoch, like a star,
Shines very bright and very far,
But nothing shall its lustre mar,
Though distant yet.

If I, in vain, must sit and wait,
To realize our future state,
I shall not be disconsolate,
My cigarette!

DOLLIE RADFORD

BEHIND a WALL

I own a solace shut within my heart,
A garden full of quaint delight
And warm with drowsy, poppied sunshine; bright,
Flaming with lilies out of whose cups dart
Shining things
With powdered wings.

Here terrace sinks to terrace, arbors close
The ends of dreaming paths; a wanton wind
Jostles the half-ripe pears, and then, unkind,
Tumbles a-slumber in a pillar rose,
With content
Grown indolent.

By night my garden is o'erhung with gems
Fixed in an onyx setting. Fireflies
Flicker their lanterns in my dazzled eyes.
In serried rows I guess the straight, stiff stems
Of hollyhocks
Against the rocks.

So far and still it is that, listening,
I hear the flowers talking in the dawn;
And where a sunken basin cuts the lawn,
Cinctured with iris, pale and glistening,
The sudden swish
Of a waking fish.

Amy Lowell

THE BLESSED DAMOZEL, *Dante Gabriel Rossetti.*

LA GHIRLANDATA, *Dante Gabriel Rossetti.*

A LOST CHORD

Seated one day at the Organ,
    I was weary and ill at ease,
And my fingers wandered idly
    Over the noisy keys.

I do not know what I was playing,
    Or what I was dreaming then;
But I struck one chord of music,
    Like the sound of a great Amen.

It flooded the crimson twilight
    Like the close of an Angel's Psalm,
And it lay on my fevered spirit
    With a touch of infinite calm.

It quieted pain and sorrow,
    Like love overcoming strife;
It seemed the harmonious echo
    From our discordant life.

It linked all perplexed meanings
    Into one perfect peace,
And trembled away into silence
    As if it were loth to cease.

I have sought, but I seek it vainly,
    That one lost chord divine,
Which came from the soul of the Organ,
    And entered into mine.

It may be that Death's bright angel
    Will speak in that chord again, –
It may be that only in Heaven
    I shall hear that grand Amen.

Adelaide Anne Procter

YOUTH

Sweet empty sky of June without a stain,
    Faint, gray-blue dewy mists on far-off hills,
Warm, yellow sunlight flooding mead and plain,
    That each dark copse and hollow overfills;
    The rippling laugh of unseen, rain-fed rills,
Weeds delicate-flowered, white and pink and gold,
A murmur and a singing manifold.

The gray, austere old earth renews her youth
    With dew-lines, sunshine, gossamer, and haze.
How still she lies and dreams, and veils the truth,
    While all is fresh as in the early days!
    What simple things be these the soul to raise
To bounding joy, and make young pulses beat,
With nameless pleasure finding life so sweet.

On such a golden morning forth there floats,
    Between the soft earth and the softer sky,
In the warm air adust with glistening motes,
    The mystic winged and flickering butterfly,
    A human soul, that hovers giddily
Among the gardens of earth's paradise,
Nor dreams of fairer fields or loftier skies.

From 'Epochs', a series of sixteen poems: 'The epochs of our life are not in the visible facts, but in the silent thought by the wayside as we walk.' Emerson

Emma Lazarus

FLORA, *Evelyn de Morgan.*

DREAMS and REALITIES

. . . that precarious Gait
Some call Experience.

EMILY DICKINSON

THE VALLEY OF SHADOWS,
Evelyn de Morgan.

I STEPPED from PLANK to PLANK

I stepped from Plank to Plank
A slow and cautious way
The Stars about my Head I felt
About my Feet the Sea.

I knew not but the next
Would be my final inch –
This gave me that precarious Gait
Some call Experience.

DESTINY, *John William Waterhouse.*

THE LADY OF SHALOTT, *William Holman Hunt.*

CROSSED THREADS

The silken threads by viewless spinners spun,
Which float so idly on the summer air,
And help to make each summer morning fair,
Shining like silver in the summer sun,
Are caught by wayward breezes, one by one,
And blown to east and west and fastened there,
Weaving on all the roads their sudden snare.
No sign which road doth safest, freest run,
The winged insects know, that soar so gay
To meet their death upon each summer day.
How dare we any human deed arraign;
Attempt to reckon any moment's cost;
Or any pathway trust as safe and plain
Because we see not where the threads have crossed?

HELEN JACKSON

TWO LOVERS

Two lovers by a moss-grown spring:
They leaned soft cheeks together there,
Mingled the dark and sunny hair,
And heard the wooing thrushes sing.
O budding time!
O love's blest prime!

Two wedded from the portal stept:
The bells made happy carollings,
The air was soft as fanning wings,
White petals on the pathway slept.
O pure-eyed bride!
O tender pride!

Two faces o'er a cradle bent:
Two hands above the head were locked;
These pressed each other while they rocked,
Those watched a life that love had sent.
O solemn hour!
O hidden power!

Two parents by the evening fire:
The red light fell about their knees
On heads that rose by slow degrees
Like buds upon the lily spire.
O patient life!
O tender strife!

The two still sat together there,
The red light shone about their knees;
But all the heads by slow degrees
Had gone and left that lonely pair.
O voyage fast!
O vanished past!

The red light shone upon the floor
And made the space between them wide;
They drew their chairs up side by side,
Their pale cheeks joined, and said, 'Once more!'
O memories!
O past that is!

George Eliot

CUPID AND PSYCHE, *Annie Swynnerton.*

WAR, *Anna Lea Merritt.*

GRIEF

I tell you, hopeless grief is passionless;
That only men incredulous of despair,
Half-taught in anguish, through the midnight air
Beat upward to God's throne in loud access
Of shrieking and reproach. Full desertness
In souls as countries, lieth silent-bare
Under the blanching, vertical eye-glare
Of the absolute Heavens. Deep-hearted man, express
Grief for thy Dead in silence like to death –
Most like a monumental statue set
In everlasting watch and moveless woe
Till itself crumble to the dust beneath.
Touch it; the marble eyelids are not wet:
If it could weep, it could arise and go.

Elizabeth Barrett Browning

REVERIE, *Dante Gabriel Rossetti.*

A SCHERZO

With the wasp at the innermost heart of a peach,
On a sunny wall out of tip-toe reach,
With the trout in the darkest summer pool,
With the fern-seed clinging behind its cool
Smooth frond, in the chink of an aged tree,
In the woodbine's horn with the drunken bee,
With the mouse in its nest in a furrow old,
With the chrysalis wrapt in its gauzy fold;
With things that are hidden, and safe, and bold,
With things that are timid, and shy, and free,
Wishing to be;
With the nut in its shell, with the seed in its pod,
With the corn as it sprouts in the kindly clod,
Far down where the secret of beauty shows
In the bulb of the tulip, before it blows;
With things that are rooted, and firm, and deep,
Quiet to lie, and dreamless to sleep;
With things that are chainless, and tameless, and proud,
With the fire in the jagged thunder-cloud,
With the wind in its sleep, with the wind in its waking,
With the drops that go to the rainbow's making,
Wishing to be with the light leaves shaking,
Or stones on some desolate highway breaking;
Far up on the hills, where no foot surprises
The dew as it falls, or the dust as it rises;
To be couched with the beast in its torrid lair,
Or drifting on ice with the polar bear,
With the weaver at work at his quiet loom;
Anywhere, anywhere, out of this room!

DORA GREENWELL

PASSING and GLASSING

All things that pass
Are woman's looking-glass;
They show her how her bloom must fade,
And she herself be laid
With withered roses in the shade;
With withered roses and the fallen peach,
Unlovely, out of reach
Of summer joy that was.

All things that pass
Are woman's tiring-glass;
The faded lavender is sweet,
Sweet the dead violet
Culled and laid by and cared for yet;
The dried-up violets and dried lavender
Still sweet, may comfort her,
Nor need she cry Alas!

All things that pass
Are wisdom's looking-glass;
Being full of hope and fear, and still
Brimful of good or ill,
According to our work and will;
For there is nothing new beneath the sun;
Our doings have been done,
And that which shall be was.

CHRISTINA ROSSETTI

THE MIRROR OF VENUS, *Edward Burne-Jones.*

Solitude

Laugh, and the world laughs with you;
  Weep, and you weep alone;
For the sad old earth must borrow its mirth,
  But has trouble enough of its own.
Sing, and the hills will answer;
  Sigh, it is lost on the air;
The echoes bound to a joyful sound,
  But shrink from voicing care.

Rejoice, and men will seek you;
  Grieve, and they turn and go;
They want full measure of all your pleasure,
  But they do not need your woe.
Be glad, and your friends are many;
  Be sad, and you lose them all, –
There are none to decline your nectared wine,
  But alone you must drink life's gall.

Feast, and your halls are crowded;
  Fast, and the world goes by.
Succeed and give, and it helps you live,
  But no man can help you die.
There is room in the halls of pleasure
  For a large and lordly train,
But one by one we must all file on
  Through the narrow aisles of pain.

Ella Wheeler Wilcox

APRIL LOVE, *Arthur Hughes.*

THE SLEEPING GIRL, *Edith Ellenborough Corbet.*

~WORN OUT~

Thy strong arms are around me, love,
   My head is on thy breast:
Though words of comfort come from thee,
   My soul is not at rest:

For I am but a startled thing,
   Nor can I ever be
Aught save a bird whose broken wing
   Must fly away from thee.

I cannot give to thee the love
   I gave so long ago –
The love that turned and struck me down
   Amid the blinding snow.

I can but give a sinking heart
   And weary eyes of pain,
A faded mouth that cannot smile
   And may not laugh again.

Yet keep thine arms around me, love,
   Until I drop to sleep:
Then leave me – saying no good-bye,
   Lest I might fall and weep.

ELIZABETH SIDDAL

PETALS

Life is a stream
On which we strew
Petal by petal the flower of our heart;
The end lost in dream,
They float past our view,
We only watch their glad, early start.

Freighted with hope,
Crimsoned with joy,
We scatter the leaves of our opening rose;
Their widening scope,
Their distant employ,
We never shall know. And the stream as it flows

Sweeps them away,
Each one is gone
Ever beyond into infinite ways.
We alone stay
While years hurry on,
The flower fared forth, though its fragrance still stays.

Amy Lowell

THE ROSE FROM ARMIDA'S GARDEN, *Marie Spartali Stillman.*

The OLD STOIC

Riches I hold in light esteem;
    And Love I laugh to scorn;
And lust of fame was but a dream
    That vanished with the morn:

And if I pray, the only prayer
    That moves my lips for me
Is, 'Leave the heart that now I bear,
    And give me liberty!'

Yes, as my swift days near their goal,
    'Tis all that I implore;
In life and death, a chainless soul,
    With courage to endure.

EMILY JANE BRONTË

THE WORSHIP OF MAMMON, *Evelyn de Morgan.*

MEDEA, *Anthony Frederick Sandys.*

I sat before my glass one day,
And conjured up a vision bare,
Unlike the aspects glad and gay,
That erst were found reflected there –
The vision of a woman, wild
With more than womanly despair.

Her hair stood back on either side
A face bereft of loveliness.
It had no envy now to hide
What once no man on earth could guess.
It formed the thorny aureole
Of hard, unsanctified distress.

Her lips were open – not a sound
Came through the parted lines of red,
Whate'er it was, the hideous wound
In silence and in secret bled.
No sigh relieved her speechless woe,
She had no voice to speak her dread.

And in her lurid eyes there shone
The dying flame of life's desire,
Made mad because its hope was gone,
And kindled at the leaping fire
Of jealousy and fierce revenge,
And strength that could not change nor tire.

Shade of a shadow in the glass,
O set the crystal surface free!
Pass – as the fairer visions pass –
Nor ever more return, to be
The ghost of a distracted hour,
That heard me whisper: – 'I am she!'

MARY ELIZABETH COLERIDGE

UP-HILL

Does the road wind up-hill all the way?
  Yes, to the very end.
Will the day's journey take the whole long day?
  From morn to night, my friend.

But is there for the night a resting-place?
  A roof for when the slow dark hours begin.
May not the darkness hide it from my face?
  You cannot miss that inn.

Shall I meet other wayfarers at night?
  Those who have gone before.
Then must I knock, or call when just in sight?
  They will not keep you standing at that door.

Shall I find comfort, travel-sore and weak?
  Of labour you shall find the sum.
Will there be beds for me and all who seek?
  Yea, beds for all who come.

CHRISTINA ROSSETTI

HOPE IN THE PRISON OF DESPAIR, *Evelyn de Morgan.*

LAST SONGS

'Tis death, the spider, in his net,
Who lures the dancers as they glide,

DORA SIGERSON SHORTER

LAUS VENERIS,
Edward Burne-Jones.

THE LOVER'S WORLD, *Eleanor Fortescue-Brickdale.*

The WATCHER in the WOOD

Deep in the wood's recesses cool
I see the fairy dancers glide,
In cloth of gold, in gown of green,
My lord and lady side by side.

But who has hung from leaf to leaf,
From flower to flower, a silken twine –
A cloud of grey that holds the dew
In globes of clear enchanted wine?

Or stretches far from branch to branch,
From thorn to thorn, in diamond rain,
Who caught the cup of crystal pure
And hung so fair the shining chain?

'Tis death, the spider, in his net,
Who lures the dancers as they glide,
In cloth of gold, in gown of green,
My lord and lady side by side.

DORA SIGERSON SHORTER

A REMINISCENCE

Yes, thou art gone! and never more
Thy sunny smile shall gladden me;
But I may pass the old church door,
And pace the floor that covers thee,

May stand upon the cold, damp stone,
And think that, frozen, lies below
The lightest heart that I have known,
The kindest I shall ever know.

Yet, though I cannot see thee more,
'Tis still a comfort to have seen;
And though thy transient life is o'er,
'Tis sweet to think that thou hast been;

To think a soul so near divine,
Within a form, so angel fair,
United to a heart like thine,
Has gladdened once our humble sphere.

Anne Brontë

PROSERPINE, *Dante Gabriel Rossetti.*

An End

Love, strong as Death, is dead.
Come, let us make his bed
Among the dying flowers:
A green turf at his head;
And a stone at his feet,
Whereon we may sit
In the quiet evening hours.

He was born in the Spring,
And died before the harvesting:
On the last warm summer day
He left us; he would not stay
For Autumn twilight cold and grey.
Sit we by his grave, and sing
He is gone away.

To few chords and sad and low
Sing we so:
Be our eyes fixed on the grass
Shadow-veiled as the years pass,
While we think of all that was
In the long ago.

CHRISTINA ROSSETTI

BY A CLEAR WELL, WITHIN A LITTLE FIELD, *Marie Spartali Stillman.*

ECHO AND NARCISSUS, *John William Waterhouse.*

I DIED for BEAUTY

I died for Beauty – but was scarce
Adjusted in the Tomb
When One who died for Truth, was lain
In an adjoining Room –

He questioned softly 'Why I failed'?
'For Beauty', I replied –
'And I – for Truth – Themself are One –
We Brethren, are', He said –

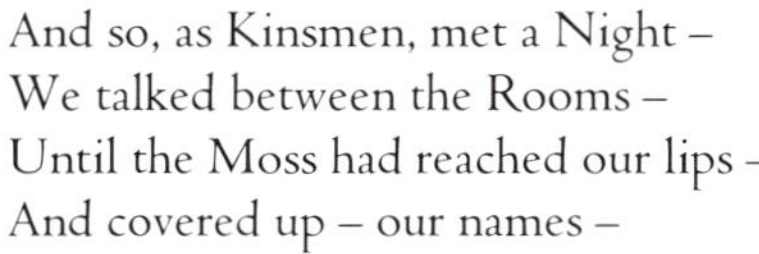

And so, as Kinsmen, met a Night –
We talked between the Rooms –
Until the Moss had reached our lips –
And covered up – our names –

EMILY DICKINSON

REMEMBRANCE

Cold in the earth – and the deep snow piled
above thee,
Far, far, removed, cold in the dreary grave!
Have I forgot, my only Love, to love thee,
Severed at last by Time's all-severing wave?

Now, when alone, do my thoughts no longer
hover
Over the mountains, on that northern shore,
Resting their wings where heath and fern-leaves
cover
Thy noble heart for ever, ever more?

Cold in the earth – and fifteen wild Decembers,
From those brown hills, have melted into spring:
Faithful, indeed, is the spirit that remembers
After such years of change and suffering!

Sweet Love of youth, forgive, if I forget thee,
While the world's tide is bearing me along;
Other desires and other hopes beset me,
Hopes which obscure, but cannot do thee wrong!

No later light has lightened up my heaven,
No second morn has ever shone for me;
All my life's bliss from thy dear life was given,
All my life's bliss is in the grave with thee.

But, when the days of golden dreams had perished,
And even Despair was powerless to destroy;
Then did I learn how existence could be cherished,
Strengthened, and fed without the aid of joy.

Then did I check the tears of useless passion –
Weaned my young soul from yearning after thine;
Sternly denied its burning wish to hasten
Down to that tomb already more than mine.

And, even yet, I dare not let it languish,
Dare not indulge in memory's rapturous pain;
Once drinking deep of that divinest anguish,
How could I seek the empty world again?

Emily Jane Brontë

A KNIGHT, *Kate Elizabeth Bunce.*

On the THRESHOLD

O God, my dream! I dreamed that you were dead;
Your mother hung above the couch and wept
Whereon you lay all white, and garlanded
With blooms of waxen whiteness. I had crept
Up to your chamber-door, which stood ajar,
And in the doorway watched you from afar,
Nor dared advance to kiss your lips and brow.
I had no part nor lot in you, as now;
Death had not broken between us the old bar;
Nor torn from out my heart the old, cold sense
Of your misprision and my impotence.

AMY LEVY

MAY MORRIS, *Dante Gabriel Rossetti.*

NIGHT WITH HER TRAIN OF STARS AND HER GREAT GIFT OF SLEEP, *Edward Robert Hughes.*

MATERNITY

One wept whose only child was dead,
New-born, ten years ago.
'Weep not; he is in bliss,' they said.
She answered, 'Even so.

'Ten years ago was born in pain
A child, not now forlorn.
But oh, ten years ago, in vain,
A mother, a mother was born.'

ALICE MEYNELL

NIGHT AND SLEEP, *Evelyn de Morgan.*

COLD and QUIET

Cold, my dear, – cold and quiet.
In their cups on yonder lea,
Cowslips fold the brown bee's diet;
So the moss enfoldeth thee.
'Plant me, plant me, O love, a lily flower –
Plant at my head, I pray you, a green tree;
And when our children sleep,' she sighed, 'at the dusk hour,
And when the lily blossoms, O come out to me!'

Lost, my dear? Lost! nay, deepest
Love is that which loseth least;
Through the night-time while thou sleepest,
Still I watch the shrouded east.
Near thee, near thee, my wife that aye liveth,
'Lost' is no word for such a love as mine;
Love from her past to me a present giveth,
And love itself doth comfort, making pain divine.

Rest, my dear, rest. Fair showeth
That which was, and not in vain:
Sacred have I kept, God knoweth,
Love's last words atween us twain.
'Hold by our past, my only love, my lover;
Fall not, but rise, O love, by loss of me!'
Boughs from our garden, white with bloom hang over.
Love, now the children slumber, I come out to thee.

JEAN INGELOW

~LAST WORDS~

Dear hearts, whose love has been so sweet to know,
That I am looking backward as I go,
Am lingering while I haste, and in this rain
Of tears of joy am mingling tears of pain;
Do not adorn with costly shrub, or tree,
Or flower, the little grave which shelters me.
Let the wild wind-sown seeds grow up unharmed,
And back and forth all summer, unalarmed,
Let all the tiny, busy creatures creep;
Let the sweet grass its last year's tangles keep;
And when, remembering me, you come some day
And stand there, speak no praise, but only say,
'How she loved us! 'T was that which made her dear!'
Those are the words that I shall joy to hear.

HELEN JACKSON

THE BELOVED, *Dante Gabriel Rossetti.*

THE CHILD ENTHRONED, *Thomas Cooper Gotch.*

YOUTH and DEATH

What hast thou done to this dear friend of mine,
Thou cold, white, silent Stranger? From my hand
Her clasped hand slips to meet the grasp of thine;
Her eyes that flamed with love, at thy command
Stare stone-blank on blank air; her frozen heart
Forgets my presence. Teach me who thou art,
Vague shadow sliding 'twixt my friend and me.
    I never saw thee till this sudden hour.
What secret door gave entrance unto thee?
    What power is thine, o'ermastering Love's own power?

AGE and DEATH

Come closer, kind, white, long-familiar friend,
    Embrace me, fold me to thy broad, soft breast.
Life has grown strange and cold, but thou dost bend
    Mild eyes of blessing wooing to my rest.
So often hast thou come, and from my side
So many hast thou lured, I only bide
Thy beck, to follow glad thy steps divine.
    Thy world is peopled for me; this world's bare.
    Through all these years my couch thou didst prepare.
Thou art supreme Love – kiss me – I am thine!

Emma Lazarus

SONG

When I am dead, my dearest,
  Sing no sad songs for me;
Plant thou no roses at my head,
  Nor shady cypress tree:
Be the green grass above me
  With showers and dewdrops wet;
And if thou wilt, remember,
  And if thou wilt, forget.

I shall not see the shadows,
  I shall not feel the rain;
I shall not hear the nightingale
  Sing on, as if in pain:
And dreaming through the twilight
  That doth not rise nor set,
Haply I may remember,
  And haply may forget.

CHRISTINA ROSSETTI

ISABELLA AND THE POT OF BASIL, *William Holman Hunt.*

~ THE POETS ~

Biographical information and text acknowledgements

ANNE BRONTË (1820–49) was the youngest of the three Brontë sisters, whose heroic struggles against isolation and poverty secured a posthumous fame that continues to attract visitors from all over the world to their remote parsonage home in the tiny Yorkshire village of Haworth. 'A Reminiscence' perhaps refers to Anne Brontë's suggested attachment to her father's curate, William Weightman, who died at the early age of 28. 'A Windy Day' (full title 'Lines Composed in a Wood on a Windy Day') expresses her characteristic delight in the freedom of nature. Both poems from *Poems by Currer, Ellis and Acton Bell* (London, 1846).

CHARLOTTE BRONTË (1816–55) is more famous as a creator of indomitable heroines than as a poet. 'The Autumn Day its Course has Run', scribbled in her German exercise book used when she was studying, teaching – and falling in love – in Brussels, shows the writer in characteristically thoughtful mood, sensitive and responsive to the natural world: transcribed from MS 118 in The Bonnell Collection, Brontë Museum, Haworth. By courtesy of the Brontë Society.

EMILY JANE BRONTË (1818–48) is outstanding both as the creator of the demoniac Heathcliff in *Wuthering Heights* and for her poetic gifts. All four surviving Brontë children wrote imaginative sagas which continued well into their adult lives. 'Remembrance' is the passionate lament of Rosina Alcona, the Queen of Gondal, for her beloved Julius, assassinated by rebels fifteen years previously but still achingly present in her memory. 'Love and Friendship': from *Wuthering Heights and Agnes Grey* by Ellis and Acton Bell, with A Selection from their Literary Remains (London, 1850); 'Remembrance' and 'The Old Stoic' from *Poems by Currer, Ellis, and Acton Bell* (London, 1846).

The clandestine love affair of ELIZABETH BARRETT BROWNING (1806–61) with the poet Robert Browning and their subsequent elopement after she had lived as an invalid for many years constitute one of the great Victorian romances. The 'Sonnets from the Portuguese' were written during Browning's courtship but not shown to him until three years after they were married. Because of their intimate and erotic content, Elizabeth Barrett Browning

published them as translations from original works written in Portuguese. 'Go From Me': from 'Sonnets from the Portuguese', Vol. III, *Elizabeth Barrett Browning's Poetical Works* (London, 1866); 'Grief' from Vol. II (op. cit.); 'The Best Thing in the World' from Vol. IV (op. cit.).

MARY ELIZABETH COLERIDGE (1861–1907) was related to the poet Samuel Taylor Coleridge. Novelist as well as poet, her poems were published in her lifetime under the pseudonym Anodos. 'The Other Side of a Mirror' was published in a slender volume in the publishers Elkin Mathews' charming 'Shilling Garland' series, and offers a surprisingly modern treatment of the problem of identity from *Fancy's Guerdon* by Anodos (London, 1897).

EMILY DICKINSON (1830–86) lived all her life at her family home in Amherst, Massachusetts. Increasingly reclusive, she wrote a substantial number of poems (almost 1800 survive), of which only a handful were published in her lifetime. On seeking advice on her work from the editor of *The Atlantic Monthly*, she was advised to make her poems more 'regular', and the complete texts with their unconventional punctuation were not published until the 1950s. Her poetry explores the 'great themes': the nature of life and death, love and friendship, and the existence of God. In form and content, they are startlingly original and reward careful re-reading. Reprinted by permission of the publishers and the Trustees of Amherst College from *The Poems of Emily Dickinson*, Thomas H. Johnson, ed., Cambridge, Mass.; The Belknap Press of Harvard University Press, Copyright 1951 (c) 1955, 1979, 1983, by the President and Fellows of Harvard College.

GEORGE ELIOT (1819–80), born Mary Anne Evans, is principally known as a great Victorian novelist. She came late to fiction, publishing her first stories when she was 37, but poetry was also an important means of expression for her. The 'Brother and Sister' series celebrates her memories of her beloved brother Isaac, from whom she was estranged for many years when she chose to live with a married man, the writer George Henry Lewes. 'Brother and Sister II' and 'Two Lovers' from *The Legend of Jubal and Other Poems, Old and New* (London, 1879).

DORA GREENWELL (1821–82) knew the poet Christina Rossetti and shared her keen interest in theology. She was an advocate of better education for intelligent women and supported the struggle for women to win the vote. Her essays and poems reflect these enthusiasms, and also explore human relationships with gentle irony. 'A Scherzo (A Shy Person's Wishes)' offers a half-humorous, half-painful description of social embarrassment and suggests a strong sympathy with the freedom and privacy of the natural world: from *Poems* (London, 1867).

Jean Ingelow (1820–97) wrote novels and children's books, as well as publishing poetry that was highly valued in her lifetime, to the extent that a group of American authors petitioned Queen Victoria to make her Poet Laureate. She knew members of the literary élite – Tennyson and Browning, as well as Christina Rossetti – but remained a shy woman who never married: 'If I had married, I should *not* have written books.' 'The Long White Seam' appeals by its simple rhythmical expression of romantic feeling: a young sailor returns home to see his betrothed sewing her wedding veil. 'Cold and Quiet' and 'The Long White Seam' from *Poems*, Vol. 2 (London, 1880).

Helen Jackson (1830–85) was born, like her friend Emily Dickinson, in Amherst, Massachusetts. She became a more public figure than Dickinson, a powerful advocate of Indian rights, and a prolific writer of articles and book reviews, although she published much of her work under masculine-sounding pseudonyms as she believed publicity was indecorous for women. She married twice, refusing her second husband until he agreed she should be completely free to explore her own interests. Her poetry was popular in her lifetime and the poems selected for this anthology show a sympathetic understanding of human character and an awareness of the unpredictability of fate. 'Crossed Threads', 'Last Words' and 'Poppies on the Wheat' from *Poems* (USA, 1895).

Emma Lazarus (1849–87) was brought up in a wealthy and cultured Jewish family in New York, but did not become an active Zionist until the Russian pogroms in the 1880s. Lines from her poem 'The New Colossus' are inscribed at the foot of the Statue of Liberty: 'Give me your tired, your poor, / Your huddled masses yearning to breathe free, . . . Send these, the homeless, tempest-tost to me, / I lift my lamp beside the golden door!' 'The Elixir', 'Youth', 'Youth and Death' and 'Age and Death' from *The Poems of Emma Lazarus*, Vol. 1 (USA, 1889).

Amy Levy (1861–89), born in Clapham, was also a Jewish poet and novelist, although her poems deal more specifically with urban themes. Her first poem was published when she was 13, and she continued to write poems and fiction until her premature death from suicide. 'On the Threshold' from *A London Plane-Tree and other Verse* (London, 1889).

Amy Lowell (1874–1925) lived the busy social life of a Boston debutante before writing her first poetry in the early 1900s. In her later work she developed Imagist forms and ideas, but the poems published here are non-experimental. They reveal her voluptuous joy in natural beauty, combined in 'Hora Stellatrix' with a daring eroticism. 'Behind a Wall', 'Hora Stellatrix' and 'Petals' from *A Dome of Many-Coloured Glass* (USA, 1912).

ALICE MEYNELL (1847–1922) and her sister Elizabeth, later Lady Butler and famous for her fine paintings of military subjects, lived mainly in Europe as children. Her first volume of poems was well-received by Ruskin and George Eliot and, with eight children to support and a meagre income, Meynell became a productive poet, essayist and journalist, including writing as Art Critic for *The Pall Mall Gazette*. She was also active in the suffragette movement. 'A Shattered Lute' and 'Maternity' from *Collected Poems of Alice Meynell* (London, 1913).

EDITH NESBIT (1858–1924) is best known for her books for children which include classic favourites such as *The Treasure Seekers* and *Five Children and It*. She and her husband Hubert Bland led a somewhat unconventional life by late Victorian standards: Edith took lovers and cared for two of her husband's 'love' children as well as three of their own, and took to her pen in order to make an income for their growing family. 'Morning Song' from *Leaves of Life* (London and USA, 1888).

ADELAIDE ANNE PROCTER (1825–64) published poems in Charles Dickens' *Household Words* under the pseudonym Mary Berwick. In his introduction to her *Legends and Lyrics*, Dickens described how, having never met his mysterious contributor, he had imagined her to be a very efficient governess, returned after many years in Italy with one family: 'my mother was not a more real personage to me, than Miss Berwick the governess became'. He was therefore astonished to discover that Miss B. was in fact the daughter of one of his closest friends and had written to him anonymously to ensure an honest response to her work. 'A Love Token' and 'A Lost Chord' from *The Complete Works of Adelaide Anne Procter* (London, 1905).

Little is known about the life of DOLLIE RADFORD (1858-?). She wrote a number of charming poems that reveal both lyric gifts and an endearing ability to laugh at herself, but even the date of her death remains obscure. 'A Novice' from *Songs and Other Verses* (London and USA, 1895).

LIZETTE WOODWORTH REESE (1856–1935) was born in a country area in Maryland which she saw grow into the city of Baltimore. For many years she taught English literature and composition, as well as publishing nine volumes of poetry, reminiscences and stories of her girlhood and an autobiographical novel. Her poetry attracts both by its lyricism and by her interest in pinpointing and communicating emotion. 'Blackberry Blossoms' and 'The Singer' from *A Handful of Lavender* (USA, 1891).

Of CHRISTINA ROSSETTI (1830–94), Virginia Woolf wrote that some of her poems 'will be found adhering in perfect symmetry when the

Albert Memorial is dust and tinsel'. Sister and sometime model to the flamboyant Pre-Raphaelite artist and poet Dante Gabriel Rossetti, Christina quietly pursued her vocation, resisting marriage and the claims of children in order to write and oversee the publication of her work. 'A Birthday', 'An End', 'Echo', 'Song' and 'Up-hill' from *Goblin Market and Other Poems* (London, 1865); 'Passing and Glassing' from *A Pageant and Other Poems* (London, 1881).

ELIZABETH SIDDAL (1829–1862) is still chiefly remembered as the flame-haired model for the Pre-Raphaelites, but she was an artist in her own right and her work is now being discovered and exhibited. The poem 'Worn Out' perhaps describes her feelings towards her husband Dante Gabriel Rossetti; their complex relationship and her hopes of developing an independent life as an artist were ended with her death from laudanum at the age of thirty-two. 'Worn Out' from *Ruskin: Rossetti: Preraphaelitism,* Papers 1854 to 1862, ed. William Michael Rossetti (London, 1899).

DORA SIGERSON SHORTER (1866–1918) was born in Dublin and continued to be fiercely patriotic after her move to London on marrying the critic and editor Clement Shorter. As well as being a substantially published poet, she was a sculptor, again focusing on Irish themes in works such as the memorial group to the patriots in the 1916 Easter Rebellion. 'The Mountain Maid' and 'The Watcher in the Wood': from *The Collected Poems of Dora Sigerson Shorter* (London, 1907).

Brought up in Wisconsin, ELLA WHEELER WILCOX (1850–1919) was an enthusiastic versifier from an early age and achieved notoriety with her *Poems of Passion,* which a Chicago publisher rejected on grounds of immorality, but which went on to sell 60,000 copies in two years. During the First World War, she toured Allied Army camps in France, reading her poetry to the troops and admonishing them on clean living. Her much-anthologised poem 'Solitude' exhibits the qualities which ensured her wide popular appeal: from *The Collected Poems of Ella Wheeler Wilcox* Vol. I (London, 1917).

INDEX
OF FIRST LINES

ACKNOWLEDGEMENTS

The editor would like to thank the following for their assistance: the staff of the Bridgeman Art Library; Richard Burns, Bury Art Gallery and Museum; Claudia Briggs, Christie's Colour Library; Sarah Colegrave, Sothebys; Sue Daly, Fine Art Photographs; Maria Leach; Sheila McGregor and Sue Parkes, Birmingham Museums and Art Gallery; Pamela Gerrish Nunn; Chris Parry, Walker Art Gallery, National Museums and Galleries on Merseyside; Penny Thompson, Russell-Cotes Art Gallery and Museum, Bournemouth; Neil Walker, Nottingham Castle Museum and City Art Gallery; Norma Watt, Castle Museum, Norwich; Kathryn White, The Brontë Society; Jane Winfrey, Phillips.

The publisher would like to thank the following museums, galleries and organisations for supplying illustrations:
BIRMINGHAM MUSEUMS AND ART GALLERY: p.24 The Keepsake, *Kate Elizabeth Bunce, 1901*; p.34 Melody (Musica), *Kate Elizabeth Bunce, ca. 1895-7*; p. 86 Medea, *Anthony Frederick Sandys, 1868.*
BRIDGEMAN ART LIBRARY: p.12 Hylas and the Nymphs, *John William Waterhouse, 1896,* Manchester City Art Gallery; p.15 Queen Eleanor and Fair Rosamund, *Evelyn de Morgan, ca. 1888,* The De Morgan Foundation, London, (hereafter abr. to DMF); p.23 Port after Stormy Seas, *Evelyn de Morgan, 1905*, DMF; p.27 Young Girl with a Garland of Marguerites, *Sophie Anderson, 1867,* Gavin Graham Gallery, London; p.29 Morgan-le-Fay, *Anthony Frederick Sandys, 1864,* Birmingham Museums and Art Gallery; p.30 The Lament, *Edward Burne-Jones, 1866,* William Morris Gallery, Walthamstow; p.33 Love's Passing, *Evelyn de Morgan, 1883-84*, DMF; p.37 Lux in Tenebris, *Evelyn de Morgan, 1895*, DMF; p.40 The Storm Spirits, *Evelyn de Morgan,* DMF; p.42 A Necklace of Wild Flowers, *Emma Sandys,* Forbes Magazine Collection, New York; p.46 The Prisoner, *Evelyn de Morgan, 1907-8*, DMF; p.53 Head of a Nymph, *Sophie Anderson,* Roy Miles Fine Paintings, London; p.55 Mariana in the Moated Grange, *John Everett Millais, 1851,* Private Collection; p.56 Il Dolce Far Niente, *William Holman Hunt, 1866,* Forbes Magazine Collection, New York; p.59 The Blessed Damozel, *Dante Gabriel Rossetti, 1871-7,* Fogg Museum of Art, Harvard; p.60 and cover La Ghirlandata, *Dante Gabriel Rossetti, 1873,* Guildhall Art Gallery, London; p.63 Flora, *Evelyn de Morgan, 1894,* DMF; p.64 The Valley of Shadows, *Evelyn de Morgan, 1899*, DMF; p.67 Destiny, *John William Waterhouse, 1900*, Towneley Hall Art Gallery and Museums, Burnley; p.68 The Lady of Shalott, *William Holman Hunt, 1889,* Manchester City Art Gallery; p.71 Cupid and Psyche, *Annie Swynnerton, exhib. 1923,* Oldham Art Gallery, Lancashire; p.74 Reverie, *Dante Gabriel Rossetti, 1868,* Christie's, London; p.77 The Mirror of Venus, *Edward Burne-Jones, 1898,* Gulbenkian Museum, Lisbon; p.79 April Love, *Arthur Hughes, 1855-6,* Tate Gallery, London; p.83 The Rose from Armida's Garden, *Marie Spartali Stillman,* Bonham's, London; p.85 The Worship of Mammon, *Evelyn de Morgan, 1909*, DMF; p.89 Hope in the Prison of Despair, *Evelyn de Morgan,* Private Collection; p.90 Laus Veneris, *Edward Burne-Jones, 1873-5,* Laing Art Gallery, Newcastle-upon-Tyne; p.92 The Lover's World, *Eleanor Fortescue-Brickdale, ca. 1905,* City of Bristol Museum and Art Gallery; p.95 Proserpine, *Dante Gabriel Rossetti, 1874,* Tate Gallery, London; p.103 May Morris, *Dante Gabriel Rossetti, 1872,* Private Collection; p.104 Night with her Train of Stars and her Great Gift of Sleep, *Edward Robert Hughes, 1912,* Birmingham Museums and Art Gallery; p.106 Night and Sleep, *Evelyn de Morgan,* DMF; p.109 The Beloved, *Dante Gabriel Rossetti, 1865-6,* Fogg Museum of Art, Harvard; p.110 The Child Enthroned, *Thomas Cooper Gotch, 1894,* Private Collection; p.113 Isabella and the Pot of Basil, *1867, William Holman Hunt,* Laing Art Gallery, Newcastle-upon-Tyne.
BURY ART GALLERY AND MUSEUM: p.72 War, *Anna Lea Merritt, 1883.*
CHRISTIE'S: p.20 Undine, *attr. to Louisa Starr Canziani, ca. 1863;* p. 80 The Sleeping Girl, *Edith Ellenborough Corbet, exhib. 1882;* p.101 A Knight, *Kate Elizabeth Bunce.*
FINE ART PHOTOGRAPHS AND LIBRARY LTD: p.16 Jolie Coeur (after Rossetti) *Marie Spartali Stillman*; p.19 The Chance Meeting, *Kate Elizabeth Bunce, 1907*; p.97 By a Clear Well, Within a Little Field, *Marie Spartali Stillman, 1883.*
NATIONAL MUSEUMS AND GALLERIES ON MERSEYSIDE: p.38 Spring (Apple Blossoms), *John Everett Millais, 1857-9,* Lady Lever Art Gallery; p.51 The Sense of Sight, *Annie Swynnerton, 1895,* Walker Art Gallery; pp.2, 98 Echo and Narcissus, *John William Waterhouse, 1903,* Walker Art Gallery.
PHILLIPS FINE ART AUCTIONEERS: p.48 Peek-a-Boo!, *Sophie Anderson.*
THE TATE GALLERY: p.45 Oure Ladye of Good Children, *Ford Madox Brown, 1847-61.*